The Etruscan Press publication of the present edition
of *Legible Heavens* has been made possible by a grant from the
National Endowment for the Arts.

NATIONAL
ENDOWMENT
FOR THE ARTS
A great nation
deserves great art.

Etruscan Press is a 501(c)(3) nonprofit organization.
Contributions to Etruscan Press are tax deductible
as allowed under applicable law.
For more information, a prospectus, or to order one of our titles,
contact us at etruscanpress@gmail.com.

LEGIBLE HEAVENS

ALSO BY H. L. HIX

POETRY
God Bless *
Chromatic *
Shadows of Houses *
Surely As Birds Fly
Rational Numbers
Perfect Hell

ARTIST'S BOOKS AND LIMITED EDITIONS
This Translucent Tissue (artist's book by Judi Ross)
The Last Hour (artist's book by Egidijus Rudinskas)
Intellectual Pleasures (limited edition by Aralia Press)

TRANSLATIONS
Estonian Elegy: Selected Poems, by Jüri Talvet, trans. with the author
The Mind Would Bear No Better, by Juhan Liiv, trans. with Jüri Talvet
On the Way Home: An Anthology of Contemporary Estonian Poetry, trans. with Jüri Talvet
A Call for Cultural Symbiosis, by Jüri Talvet, trans. with the author
City of Ash, by Eugenijus Ališanka, trans. with the author

ARTIST CATALOGS
Jason Pollen
Kyoung Ae Cho

ANTHOLOGIES
New Voices: Contemporary Poetry from the United States
Wild and Whirling Words: A Poetic Conversation *

THEORY AND CRITICISM
As Easy As Lying: Essays on Poetry *
Understanding William H. Gass
Understanding W. S. Merwin
Spirits Hovering Over the Ashes: Legacies of Postmodern Theory
Morte d'Author: An Autopsy

* Also published by Etruscan Press.

LEGIBLE HEAVENS

H. L. Hix

etruscan press

Etruscan Press
Wilkes University
84 West South Street
Wilkes-Barre, PA 18702
www.etruscanpress.org

10 9 8 7 6 5 4 3 2 1

Printed in the United States of America

Publishers Cataloging-in-Publication
    Hix, H. L.
        Legible heavens / H.L. Hix. -- 1st ed.
        p. cm.
        Poems.
        ISBN-13: 978-0-9797450-4-1
        ISBN-10: 0-9797450-4-7

      I. Title.

     PS3558.I88L44 2008   811'.54
                        QBI08-600246

Designed by Nicole DePolo

Etruscan Press is committed to preserving ancient forests and natural resources.
We elected to print this title on 30% post consumer recycled paper, processed
chlorine free. Etruscan Press made this paper choice because our printer,
Thomson-Shore, Inc., is a member of Green Press Initiative, a non-profit
program dedicated to supporting authors, publishers, and suppliers in their
efforts to reduce their use of fiber obtained from endangered forests.

For more information, visit www.greenpressinitiative.org

Acknowledgments

I am grateful to the editors who gave ward in the following journals to portions of this book, sometimes in versions different from those that appear here:

Alabama Literary Review	"of the several reasons…"
	"I have tried…"
	"I thirst for god…"
Bat City Review	"I've been taking…"
The Eleventh Muse	"Lineage"
	"Spoken to Judas Thomas, Jesus' Twin"
Margie	"If I overhear…"
	"Beatitudes"
Paris Review	"If silhouetted…"
Penguin Review	"kiss your fingers…"
	"when someone broke in…"
	"some nights I awaken…"
Perihelion	"Kerygma"
	"Zacchaeus the Teacher, Shamed"
	"Light"
Poetry	"If sixteenth-century Iznik ware…"
	"If the Lena River…"
	"If a Babylonian…"
	"If the maple…"
Provincetown Arts	"If on safari…"
	"If in a row…"
	"If sunlight…"
32 Poems	"Miracles"
Yale Review	"If the tattooed woman…"
	"If even under the pine…"

The opening and closing sections of "Star Chart for the Rainy Season" originated as a collaborative project with artist Eleanor Droll, and stand partner to her print "Spirits of the Rain." "All the One-Eyed Boys in Town" participated in a collaborative project with artist Doug Russell. "Beatitudes" enjoyed presentation as a holiday keepsake from Michael Peich at Aralia Press.

The epigraphs, in order of their appearance, come from: G. W. Leibniz, "Notes on Some Comments by Michel Angelo Fardella"; G. W. Leibniz, "Primary

Truths"; Slavoj Žižek, *The Ticklish Subject*; Bruno Latour, *Iconoclash*; Irving M. Copi, *Logic*; Martin Heidegger, *Being and Time*; Muriel Rukeyser, *The Life of Poetry*.

Not all the loves toward whom these songs lean can be named, but "Material Implication" speaks — with gratitude — of and to Kate.

"Star Chart for the Rainy Season" opens with passages from the biblical Song of Songs, and closes with a sentence from Augustine. The brief Spanish passage comes from the twelfth of Neruda's *Twenty Love Poems and a Song of Despair*.

"Synopsis" engages, in addition to the canonical gospels, The Protevangelium of James, The Arabic Infancy Gospel, The Infancy Gospel of Thomas, The Strasbourg Fragment, a fragment from The Preaching of Peter in Gregory of Nazianzus, an agraphum from Origen, The Acts of John, The Acts of Thomas, The Narrative of Joseph of Arimathea, Vindicta Salvatoris, and the Letter of Herod to Pilate. My source for the extracanonical texts was J. K. Elliott's *The Apocryphal New Testament* (Oxford Univ. Press, 1993).

Though since altered by various regimens and ministrations, "All the One-Eyed Boys in Town" began as a cento sequence, one section collaged from each of the following (works I insisted on thinking of as) poetic sequences: John Ashbery, *Shadow Train*; Anne Carson, *The Beauty of the Husband*; Debra Di Blasi, *Drought*; Rachel Blau DuPlessis, *Drafts 1-38: Toll*; Carol Frost, *Abstractions*; Forrest Gander, *Torn Awake*; Louise Glück, *The Wild Iris*; Donald Hall, *The One Day*; Jim Harrison, *Letters to Yesenin*; Anthony Hecht, *Flight Among the Tombs*; Lyn Hejinian, *My Life*; John Hollander, *Powers of Thirteen*; Susan Howe, *Pierce-Arrow*; Richard Kenney, *The Evolution of the Flightless Bird*; Yusef Komunyakaa, *Talking Dirty to the Gods*; Ben Lerner, *The Lichtenberg Figures*; Timothy Liu, *Hard Evidence*; David Markson, *Wittgenstein's Mistress*; Dionisio D. Martinez, *Climbing Back*; Carole Maso, *Aureole*; Alice Notley, *The Descent of Alette*; Eric Pankey, *Reliquaries*; D. A. Powell, *Tea*; Thomas Rabbitt, *The Booth Interstate*; Leslie Scalapino, *Considering how exaggerated music is*; Mark Strand, *Dark Harbor*; Ellen Bryant Voigt, *Kyrie*; Anne Waldman, *Marriage: A Sentence*; Rosmarie Waldrop, *The Reproduction of Profiles*; C. K. Williams, *Tar*; David Wojahn, *Mystery Train*; C. D. Wright, *Deepstep Come Shining*; Jay Wright, *Boleros*; Jan Zwicky, *Wittgenstein Elegies*.

TABLE OF CONTENTS

STAR CHART FOR THE RAINY SEASON   1

ALL THE ONE-EYED BOYS IN TOWN   9

Breezes sing   11
the song of sufficient reason   12
Tell me what this means   13
The heart   14
unmaking a willow   15
insinuates this: 16
dark water surrounding   17
this climate of extremes   18
some larger logic   19
that outwaits all the   20
varying light   21
It happened this way: 22
too many pieces   23
exchanged for blooms   24
changed back into   25
sparrows at their dust-baths   26
There is no avoiding   27
weariness in judgment   28
complications of meaning   29
all the switchbacks between your body and   30
the opposite hills   31
This shrine built from   32
the storm itself   33
the forbidden dissonance   34
in your eyes   35
is more true than   36
brief familiarity   37

clouded with flowers 38

Think of my body as 39

ravished, needy music 40

from birds 41

rising and falling out of 42

winter morning light 43

Imagine my life legible 44

MATERIAL IMPLICATION 45

If on safari one may see... 47

If in a row of tract houses... 48

If sixteenth-century Iznik ware... 49

If the Lena River courses north... 50

If I overhear, interrupted... 51

If sunlight reflecting off... 52

If silhouetted by sunset... 53

If even under the pine whose roots... 54

If a Babylonian astronomical diary... 55

If the maple in the neighbor's yard... 56

If after her sixth pair of tusks... 57

If the tattooed woman ahead of me... 58

SYNOPSIS 59

According to H. 61

The Mother of the Mother of God 62

From Mary's Childhood 63

Lineage 64

One Approach 66

One Sparrow 67

Zacchaeus the Teacher, Shamed 68

Beatitudes 70

Light 71

Miracles 72

Parables 73

Agrapha 77

Kerygma 78

Mercies 79

Hymn 80

Spoken to Judas Thomas, Jesus' Twin 82

Passions 83

Letter 85

Conclusion 88

Protevangelium 89

God clearly and distinctly sees the universe as implied and inscribed.

God from the beginning constituted both the soul and the body with such wisdom and such workmanship that, from the first constitution or notion of a thing, everything that happens through itself in the one corresponds perfectly to everything that happens in the other....

STAR CHART FOR THE RAINY SEASON

We are dealing here with a logic which includes its own failure in advance.

I thirst for god as a doe thirsts for the flowing stream.

The skies sing god's glory, the heavens her handiwork.
Day speaks to day, one night shares knowledge with the next.
With no need of tongue, god's song shades the earth,
wedding baldachin for the sun and his lucent bride.

Daughters of the holy city, spirits of the rain,
guard my love's sleep until her own desire rouses her.

My mourning dove, call your falling notes from the ramage,
for your dark eyes lull me, your voice soothes like cool night rain.
Seal your heart with my heart, knot your legs and arms with mine,
for love is stronger than death, and passion more fierce.
Heavy rain cannot quench love, nor flood wash it away.

•   •

kiss your fingers then touch my cheek let that be story enough
why pretend to be complete when we are not now and will not be again
when we see now we were never complete even when we thought we were
even when we took completion for granted not knowing enough
to think differently not knowing enough to think of completion at all
why fret incompletion when one of you is enough why fret age
when who among us is young

who has not done once what she never does
who has not acted out her incompletion in ways another might need
whose cheek I ask you whose cheek has loss's kissed fingers not touched

•

I've tried to find a way to tell you what I don't know how to say
something about a rooftop garden with ornamental trees
organizing the gridded gravel roofs around it lending to the view
from this room I've never been in some quality I know not to name
though naming it *hope* would lurch toward the thing I would be thinking
if I knew how to think what I know I want to think

                                        if I could think
as dogwood petals think releasing light for their beautiful few days
calling to birds that haven't lived here since before the tree's seed split
since before you ushered me out of my last life which I now know was not a life
but had gardens on the ground into this life which is no more a life than the other
though the gardens here grow brighter and smaller and higher
almost above the birds the dogwoods no longer know how to call
though call them they must these birds that know what to say and say it insistently
the birds I no longer know how to name though they be as vivid

                                        as gold
and scarlet and indigo hidden in these trees as they would be held in my hands

•

I've been taking buses lately and elevators thinking if I ride them often enough
one time I will enter a different history
                        the history in which I touch you again
in which I *can* touch you again unlike this history of once will have to be enough
in which I have learned the routes and stops so well the drivers nod when I board
know me by the name I give them to pretend this history differs somehow
from the one in which I know the buildings so well the clerks and hygienists smile
thinking I work on some floor near theirs
                        the one in which bellhops greet me
thinking me a frequent guest on some business other than imagining myself
into a city with a bus that might carry you an elevator you might ride
a city that might as well be a different world that offers a different history
than the one I inhabit the one I share with you only in buses and elevators
that seam cities I see in this history once every thirty-nine years

4

•

when someone broke in I cried out and awoke from the dream
but of course no one was there
                              which makes the dream like my life
because I wake up now at night thinking you into the room and always it is 2:30
and the woman who lives below me must hear me cry out as she would hear us
the walls are thin if you were here which you are not no matter what she thinks
or what I think and you will not be here again though my crying out in the dream
and my tumbling from it be ways to call you from one dream into the next

                    •

some nights I awaken caressing myself running my fingernails lightly
backward across my ribcage touching the tender parts of one arm
as lightly as I can with the fingertips that end the other arm
as if I were carrying signals star to star across the constellation you carry
sometimes I wake up in ways and at times and for reasons I never did before
not dreaming so much as thinking not thinking so much as longing
writing these love letters
                    let me call them what they are
                                        out of my sleep
these doves released to cross the waves toward the receding horizon
not expecting evidence of land exactly but to honor its memory

                    •

I've been rising early to meet you here in the park where the rain seldom stops
because the clouds that blow in from the sea can't cross these mountains
though I know you haunt the part of the park I've been afraid to enter
fearing I would not find my way out and anyway I knew you had left
a few lives ago lives long before mine which after all is hardly a life
and I knew my reasoning was wrong because what reasoning is not

I didn't expect to find you or find myself here in this light
that the not-quite-constant rain carries down from wherever the clouds found it
in the shadows of trees older than the places of your even-closer-to-constant pain
or what would be shadows if these trees taller than my listening for you
were not smothered under hand-urgent clouds now as always
if this brilliance didn't seem to seep up from the earth itself
if my logic did not so swiftly so finally fall apart
                                        this logic I keep mistaking for love
as a boy frightened from sleep mistakes shadows thrown by passing cars for wolves
love that I've learned is lonelier than its absence lonelier than these gasping trees
are graceful in the rain that sounds like your voice I came here wanting to hear
because pain is more beautiful than logic more beautiful than my image
of these mountains which because clouds always cover them
I know of only when you tell me they are there in that voice I've come here
where I don't live to hear
                        all this distance from where I normally don't live
which never had mountains though it always has clouds
and which does not have your voice that after all I have heard only once
and don't expect to hear ever again though here I am at the park
not exactly thinking I would find you having found so little of what I've ever sought
but listening anyway lost in spite of myself trying to reason my way out
with logic I know is faulty but which I follow because it sounds like your voice
and because so often I feel like a boy afraid to cry for fear the shadows
will hear and enforce their logic which would keep me from this park
where though I know you are not here I still listen for your voice

                .   .

of the several reasons I distrust movies the foremost is that in them
the characters do the reckless thing and come to regret what they have done

but I regret nothing having done nothing worth regret nothing reckless ever
having realized so little of my will having flown over my desires as a bird migrates
over water whose end it cannot see

                               emigran y huyen pájaros que dormían en tu alma
I regret all and only what I have not done what I failed to do failed always from some
deeper failing since each of my failings so many I no longer try to name them
each is deeper than the last

                        my failings hold one another up as the planets and stars
hold one another in orbit so here I am failing again looking down on my desires
that reach to both horizons and call each other by your name

      •   •

Finding loans more pleasure to labored seeking;
indirection stimulates the seeker's hunger.
God grants truth only to desire.

ALL THE ONE-EYED BOYS IN TOWN

The whole series has meaning, but none of its elements has any sense.

to flatten your portrait of god, to make it plain

and to hear colors at night,
why not confess to restless
rivulets? **Breezes sing** in
coded sequence, the path loves
the forest or pities it,
when earth crusts forth oracle
my fears echo as your voice.
All oaks mimic this oak: black,
unsatisfactory as
love, worn down more by each rain.
It doesn't matter, the world.
No one saw room in my guilt
for your lush, wild elegance.

It's like watching a movie of reasoning, this

incomplete explanation, this relationship

    breathing your body over
    all nine of my fingertips.
    Like rain improvising, I
    traced **the song of sufficient**
    reason down your spine. Swallows
    stopped circling, but not desire,
    whose terror proves to me, love,
    that those cold swift streams we ran
    were not rivers at all. Not
    musician enough to stunt
    the grammatical, I'm left
    listening for lost moments,
    their improbabilities

    of sequence imposing episodes between you

and what shines. Only after my tongue was cut out

        could I ride my nightmare through
        garden-given gaspings, seeds
        floating in seawater, one
        death to another. **Tell me**
        what this means, our fall, your tongue
        and clitoris, swollen with
        something halted, wrong acres
        brailled with a wisping of down.
        Did someone spell this sequence
        as breath-weight alonenesses,
        these petals flustered to earth?
        Gods ignite themselves like snow.
        I desire you, every seam

        and flounce of you, sentenced into the languages

I speak out of my sleep, having dreamed them whole. I'll

  let you cry. I've cried too much.
  The heart ajar, born wounded,
  buys its crusts with begged-for coins.
  Sequence hums, asserts again
  its strict melody. Maybe
  the soul *is* shared. An atoll,
  its little sunken island.
  She bled doubt out. He stole through
  one world but not her others.
  It's hot, yes, but we're not here
  for long, suffocated by
  such exquisite reds, yellows,
  greens, so marginal and frail.

  We locked the doors — remember? — and let our lovers

become less real, less urgent, less moonscarred and gnarled.

But what sings from water-clear,
sequenced, sufficient wonder,
cigarette smoke, spent tea bags,
a never-was-golden day,
will cover all our losses:
those five-dollar-a-week rooms,
no one to name us, to risk
the breath train from Leningrad,
swans **unmaking a willow**
by the river, women in
succulent undergarments,
past love but not love poems
recited in bright deserts.

Everywhere you've hovered before, I meant to stand

while lights went out in the valley below. So what

       if bright-bellied winter stars
       nap overhead? The body
       insinuates this: ashes
       defining diaspora,
       others' wars floodlit, crimson
       confessions, wine-hued dreams that
       tint dispassionate linens,
       turn back the curved listless world
       that sequences what I know
       I can't save? Your knees, my pulse,
       notes you meant not to be heard.
       Touch me, but if not your breath
       will do, equal parts patience

       and worry, watching October lilt to its rest,

feeling christened, swept insistently through bee-flustered

      goldenrod. All night that square
      imprisoned by lights blown black.
      Let me explain what I mean.
      Something forbidden and lean
      is induced in me by your
      hands, your hair, the flow of your
      back, **dark water surrounding**
      our floating hold, by lilies,
      the listings of a going
      of geese. I was calling your
      names. You seemed to be swimming
      further and further into
      the sequence. I followed far

      enough to let your quickened pulse for the first time

fill the spaces of my stammering, fill all its

        palsied silences, fill small
        wings' blurred transparence, the dim,
        indeterminate sequence
        of my seeing. My inept,
        yearning hands harvest blighted
        reports on star-scarved twilights.
        In **this climate of extremes**
        all my weary faces ask
        what hand burined birds, etched them
        as hesitant crossings-out
        of comprehensive darkness,
        lustrousness burned into
        that resist, our histories.

        If I've lost those pictures of you I never had,

if consciousness hid them, what assurance of touch

       incandesces this cosmos
       of integumentations,
       guesses, sequences, theses.
       Bewildered ghosts who still thirst,
       who still desire the spare life
       bleak north sings itself raw for,
       these birds, small blue things betrayed,
       wrapped in their rivers of silk,
       hope, like me, to tell of night,
       unmeant thoughts imposed on sleep
       that frame **some larger logic**
       than explicates the body.
       This uninhibited room,

       a penalty paid for grammar, inclines our thought

to premonitions invisible but present.

These lisped and stuttered listings
emaciate me the way
limping arabesques of dust
unravel things here: stray stars,
bland luck, dirt road headed home,
earth tones and siennas, sleep,
its detail-strewn turbulence
proof that memory cheats truth.
The process calls for distance,
satellite footage, bodies
terrible petals snowing
all night into a landscape
that outwaits all the skewed girls.

Sequence healed our war-poisoned earth by alchemy

as if somewhere a fire-fostered sister sequence

      meant to insist on strange stars'
      varying light. Imagine
      all this otherwise, give it
      your own sense-distorted twist:
      unaccountable yellows,
      red delicacies wild as
      lovers quarreling over
      how it was for the short span
      of their mutual dream. Let
      trees try resisting the wind,
      let storms leave their earth-spiced air,
      their stored light as recompense
      for my disfigurement. All

      winter your hands feel lies. Everything threatens snow,

though I still insist intelligence is latticed,

        quartz-clastic and quarantined,
        unfazed by enormities
        measured by matchlight as frail
        as falcon-call and as fierce,
        untouched by your voice listing
        sequences of mysteries:
        teal in marsh reeds one sun-shot
        morning, drops on a woodstove,
        a swift surprise of minnows.
        Baffled by great migrations,
        I drowse away each winter.
        It happened this way: your name
        overcame the only world

I had imagined. The lonely face of god strayed

through the redwoods, disguised as mandalas dusted

on moths' wings. Sunlight sequenced
sandstone hills. I admit
I'm still afraid of faces.
There are **too many pieces**
to my idea, I must
be someone else. All those strings
imply terrible distance.
The trees encase all the most
interesting words, birds' fears,
ecstasies of rock, numbers'
stutter, the years' logic lost
to inattention. I want
rhythm to match the unveiled:

fenceposts covered with moss, entire tall hollyhocks

overcome with their own color. Not everyone

        prays for fire. Some souls linger
        with griefs under cold cinders
        where they belong, weeds and ashes
        suffocating them as skies
        suffocate cities, force on
        them the rules of rule. When she
        fell asleep, my life began
        building this house which does not
        exist, in the valley of
        long shadows. Apparently
        I want to sequence myself,
        kneel down to drink error from
        a ditch gray with grass, with bribes

        I **exchanged for blooms** like small spent faces. I tried

to handle hard necessities first, to become

        a bird, preferably an owl
        because it stays so dark here
        where her dreams rain on my dreams,
        and all withdraw to the woods,
        all the third things together.
        Once the flowers withered, I
        changed back into my lost self.
        Here are my tears, jeweled blue.
        My shadows plan to return
        to places no god would know,
        where these sequences begin.
        I want to invent loss; am
        I really the only one?

        That colder, deeper, unilluminated place,

nightshade's nectar and dark, undid my flesh with yours.

    The shadowy street, rain blown
    down this rubbled wynd, wet soot
    staining my love's carved name gray:
    all corruptions tungsten-tinged.
    Dark, dishonorable scars
    from my trial suicides
    inhale brevity from your
    dissolving sequences. It
    did not last, our happiness.
    What passes passes swiftly:
    roofs of short-tempered cities,
    your sorrowful eyes (**sparrows
    at their dust-baths**), my embrace,

    your troubled sleep, my world leveled by my yearning,

awash with blushing textures, your hips, lipped lilies,

    sex as song. I feel lost here
    with just sequence to correct
    my view. Against so much glass
    starlight shuts a harsh door. On
    this my tentative guitar
    to tell by touch the passage
    to the river is to feel,
    obliquely on your body,
    the light. The airs I sing all
    long for feathers. **There is no**
    avoiding oblivion,
    even for embodied gods,
    horses grazing side by side.

    The hand that anticipated everything —

shining lamps lined along empty streets, our naked

        bodies, brief insect-covered
        moons, waiting without hope for
        hope, trees lost from one numbered
        forest, some ineffable
        decorum, nashki of waves
        sheened across the possible —
        heard **weariness in judgment,**
        its call-down of cirrus wisps
        scrimshawed on beach-bleached femur.
        There's no logic to my loves:
        your figure, grass in the shade,
        sleep, the sea, pelicans' wings,
        sequence itself, silver and

        frozen. Once the song ends, the sung-of world resumes

its **complications of meaning**, silence awash

      with tunnel-damp graffiti,
      junctured by saturation.
      These fragments are ghost pieces,
      ashes drifted down denser
      than mountain fog or sea spray.
      They are made by strict method,
      old newspapers blown across
      a field, seepage and stipple,
      landscapes pocked pink with foxgloves.
      Conspicuous sequences
      bear inverse enormities
      of fractions numbered past the
      edge of sensibility

      and dust this glassed-in space I keep trying to name

for the clear air overhead, its pearl-perfect

        impossibility too
        beautiful to leave alone.
        I tell complicated lies,
        illuminations brought back
        from the fields as quail feathers
        gathered to make you new wings.
        I had to leave my known life
        to map out **all the switchbacks**
        between your body and god.
        Until sequences fit, we
        trace and retrace our dirt lines.
        Your body, so nearly free,
        pulls me backward from the shore,

        salts the air with gulls' calls. Once I thought in terms of dwarf pines and yellowing valley and quiet pond,

I tried to replace my life
with red-bent light, wind rising,
earth surrendering moisture
to parched sky without concern.
What good does sequence do us
beyond spilling chilled brothers
from this tiny house, these rooms
gracelessly sliding away?
When she mistakes rain for love,
he hides his desire to fly
from the euclidean fear
rising slowly just beyond
the opposite hills. Suppose

their story ends suddenly, suddenly insists

it's enough, this strewn straw holding mud to the path,

wind jeweled juniper-blue.
Let me re-state the question.
What bends light, if cliffs of sleet
bend willows down to water?
One brittle stick above snow
holds sequence in place. **This shrine
built from** sleep's gauze of moth-dust,
its nest of misplaced relics,
beckons angels to rustle
your other body to song.
I take liberties with names,
almanacs and star charts, lace
(cousin to the dragonflies),

and still you list with reticence, imitating

not **the storm itself** but its offices. I hear

        your singing, something to do
        with sunlight, with the first signs
        of thaw, the sky from inside,
        bare trees' black calligraphy,
        a calling-out bent once then
        bent again, burned-out beach homes
        outlining sand, the first snow
        been and gone, water brought up
        from the spring, a boat adrift,
        last lilies bent, breeze-blistered
        to their inevitable
        dismantling. I lose track,
        being lonely, old, and mad.

        I am that stretch of spurred sequence inside closed doors

that block the night from the night. In love with sagebrush

and sandalwood, your body's
gift of spice-scented prayers,
I sing hymns informed by mango
and lotus blossom, your glow
of almonds, plums, salty air.
I am descanting on you,
musical, invented one.
I avalanche at your touch,
frenzied descent to sequence,
the forbidden dissonance
of luminous afternoon.
In all my imaginings
I imagine your body,

rosy pearl and word. Lost in brilliant blinding need,

I hold the smell of intuition, its call to

       spiritual erasure.
       What I know counts for nothing:
       grease, crushed clover underfoot,
       saffron and complicity,
       such ancient desperations.
       If there was a dream, it's gone.
       I see, looking **in your eyes**,
       some primitive source of grace
       traced already in the words
       I was saying as I was
       saying them, gone that moment
       of irresistible dusk,
       coal dust tracked across coal dust.

       l keep trying to sequence this loss, but it seems

an algebraic question, of no use to me.

     We make ourselves cry. There are
     no rules for sequence except
     your tears, the trees in your voice,
     those rain-laden souls lit like
     the silk curve of your cheekbones,
     hesitation, just enough
     long-ago to keep my hope
     layered and elusive. Rugs,
     hardwood, lamps, your cigarettes.
     Look hard. What **is more true than**
     the smell of that dusty road
     my soul, poor bird, spilled like grain?
     I love what shines in one twitch

     of winter twilight, unshielded in this world of

counterfeited starshine: deer twisted by headlights,

brief familiarity
gradually unraveled,
history past polaroid.
My lust for memory cooled,
but still I wake carrying
those woods in my head. I once
felt you speak to me, felt you
make of my fingers the truth,
reinvent my hands with your
wounded body, meadows grown
yellow-brown, dusted dry with
goldenrod. Outside the world
that you alone believe in,

nothing is not sequence. In this world I am yours,

entirely contained by your gaze. All things that don't

           belong to me flourish: rain,
           buttercups lamenting bird-
           laden maples, high summer,
           sequence **clouded with flowers**,
           your face, your voice, your fingers.
           Are you close enough to hear
           this my slanted life arc from
           solitude to solitude?
           Whatever else you taught, you
           taught me to grieve, to recall
           all choirs of small things, infant
           ghosts in apple trees, roses
           crusted with light. You couldn't

           know how your belly unburdens me of the world,

unthinks my voiced world to moonlight fled underground.

      Think of my body as a
      system of substitutions,
      a burning of dreams taken
      too far, a miserable
      progression from snow to sand,
      sequencing substituted
      for adequate theory,
      lace unwoven by lightning,
      methodology postponed,
      small birds shrilling my decline,
      declensions in shrill bird-rows.
      I can't remember now
      why the sky is such pale blue.

      l refuse to be forgiven, I don't want to

ask for assurance. The planet, intensified

        by contagion and chaos,
        the cocked dangers of contact,
        abandoned bombed-out places.
        Strange semaphores argue for
        these sequential lustrations,
        her **ravished, needy music**.
        In her terror for love she
        wants other solar systems
        and a former century.
        Rain, poor orphan, spirals from
        skies forgiven by eclipse.
        Let me ask you a question:
        how will bodies give account

        of the coughed provocations of architecture,

the wish-ticking of rough sacred ruins, layered

> on past layers, beyond grief,
> murdered meticulously?
> While the victims freed themselves
> **from birds** and their absences,
> my body learned that the tips
> of your fingers regulate
> hurricanes. They know the small
> serious difference between
> pour and spill, they can sustain
> a leaf floating on a pond.
> My topic is refraction,
> but ghost names will not sequence
> legibly. I remember

more about some birds than about my wife's body

in the embrace her suffering no longer longed for.

       This loss-laced life has taught me
       to reconstruct salvation
       of and in the body, with
       ice crucial to a weather-
       broken barn, the lean gone moon,
       the sparrow's demanding song.
       I find new dispensation
       in your shoulders. Sequences
       rising and falling out of
       rebuilt dreams disclose your flight.
       You promise emerald light.
       I write you the math of my
       thousand longings, the fertile

       kindling impermanence of unfamiliar names,

brush of your hands, a phrase, this world's hollow logic,

        our eternity of need.
        You say reeds form no system,
        I say souls spill as sand spills.
        Who cannot follow the flight
        of birds spread like breath
        cannot mimic, in the sweet
        winter morning light, star-fall,
        echoes, constellated shells.
        Imagine sequential light
        isolated from your names,
        those insistences whose bones,
        broken, reach heavenward for
        some harder truth, a voice

against which to measure this world's every wound,

long-shadowed space, each leaf-kiss, those fragmentary

outlines we call the real world,
music, thought. **Imagine my
life legible** to others,
crystallizing into quartz,
a match scratched down your wingbones.
Is love a mistranslation,
your face to my affections?
The question you keep asking
resists my poor dust-crusted
calculus, its rules structured
with rushed singularities,
pendant flowers, jade beads,
wrens, the storm wheeling over

my life. To consider the whole of the sequence,

MATERIAL IMPLICATION

A conditional statement asserts that its antecedent implies its consequent. It does not assert that its antecedent is true, but only that if its antecedent is true then its consequent is true also. It does not assert that its consequent is true, but only that its consequent is true if its antecedent is true.

We call the specific bringing near of what is taken care of by interpreting it circumspectly *deliberation*. The schema peculiar to it is "if-then."

**If on safari one may see
a bare-faced go-away bird
or lilac-breasted roller,
and if weaverbirds, flagrant
as goldfinches, fill flame trees
with nests like felted fruit, then**

I reject less refractory logic.
I name you Thetis of the shining breasts,
not because, windshield-warmed mornings, sun-slick,
they out-round round earth's runway-graded easts,
not for some angry, doomed, half-human son,
not for your water-life (snowy egret,
cattails, dragonfly), not for those seven
years we waited, regret kissing regret.
One lost sock. What matters goes its own way.
Someone downstreet sawing, someone's neighbor
limping her dog. Dog-hued sawdust terrain
on Mars. Everything I failed to tell her,
or just failed. My impotence to explain.
Dog-warm water-like light. Non sequitur.

If in a row of tract houses
that grid the descent into Cleveland,
a dump truck parked diagonally
occupies a whole front yard, then

a woman bows, turns her back to the wind,
feeds hatchlings in her nested hands, warms them
with her breath, but it's so hot this far end
of spring she must be lighting a Salem
instead, three blood-crusted purple knuckles,
and yes, she exhales, turns, and walks again,
her gait possessing me — everything does —
with another woman as scarred, as thin.
But all that falls as rain tonight will rise
as heat-haze tomorrow when the winds die.
It must be radical contingencies
we call love, the provisionality
of *everything* we call our lives, *bodies*
those Greeks called gods, naked under that sky.

If sixteenth-century Iznik ware
dug up in Damascus consists
of fine white clay mixed with ground quartz, then

how you slip off your shoes, heel to instep,
left foot first, leaving them to form a T,
matters no more, is no more mine to keep,
than two snow shovels still outside, ready,
as drizzle washes June into July
and trims the highway this one afternoon
with strings of headlights, no more than the way
the robin broods, wings spread out, to keep rain
from the eggs, the way her nest rapunzels
its longer, light-colored strands, how water
turns rust from red to brown on the wheelwells
of the plumber's spavined van, the clatter
that damned raccoon makes at night when he spills
the trash. But I will watch you, no matter.

If the Lena River courses north
farther than the Mississippi south,
draining Yablonovyy mountain snow
into the ice-laced Laptev Sea, then

somewhere her eyes' hue must have a rival.
In the geothermal prehistory
of pressure under what became Brazil,
in the igneous light sharp-sifted by
its facet-concentrated chronicle.
In something luminous deep undersea.
In the kincob that confesses quetzal
careening through light-karsted canopy.
Or widow's-mite-given onto insects:
a beetle's back prism-tilled minutely;
dragonfly's hexamitos-thrilled thorax;
crushed on my windshield as I drove away,
desire that kept glowing against the dusk,
star-sistered weeping that had been firefly.

If I overhear, interrupted
by breeze-roused leaves and windchimes,
a woman across the street say
into her cellphone *Why the hell*
she ain't say hi back, then and *His face*
covered with lipstick and all that shit
and *She be talkin bout she look good*
in skirts and I say Uh-uh, then

list your desires, I'll assert your sorrows,
glossed by geese in whose v grief is given,
the marred, moored one-note chorale they compose,
those lost children named again and again,
by the unbreakable fractal code
ferns signal not to us or each other
but to what means mushroom, what suggests shade
and spring, the abstract will that maths feathers,
that occasions the blue-shade-layered hills,
the dread red-shouldered hawk's shagged, haggard head,
missing moss-loosened tiles in the tunnels,
wind-washed sand-white bark-bare branches long dead,
the goose-shade of clouds any breath-blue calls,
the luminous fate coding me, dust-red.

If sunlight reflecting off
the chrome trim of the '48 Ford
in the driveway next door and passing
at a severe angle through the panes
of hundred-year-old glass in my
rented second-story room
makes shivers of light on the wall
that twist the way locust limbs twist, then

thus should the garden have flourished: roses'
reticence the least of it, melting snow
spreading pollen fallen from auroras
south across anthered plains in mud's flood-flow,
the sandhill cranes accosting Nebraska,
one for one with their doubles, flamingoes
on Nakuru, puffins in Alaska,
each spring peonies the sun séances.
Might have, had I not failed to make it so,
had I felt fewer undiscovered moons
tugging at the tides, fewer fish below
color confined to cool, lime-constant rooms,
had I not heard, seventeen years ago,
cicadas assault each other's one sense.

If silhouetted by sunset
an Amish horse and wagon cross
a bridge over the interstate,
heading north at their own pace, then

I name you Miranda for the wonder
of striped wings, nighthawks that until today
I had not seen hunting since the first year
of my last life, my lost life, now a stray
learning to scavenge after begging failed.
Nothing but totems left me now to mark.
Those birds, that dog, and you — Miranda — lisled
and legible, husk of hunger and work.
I assert you antidote, miracle
of pawprints, proof raccoons pray to the lake,
of four wild turkeys ruthing cornstubble,
of acorns making their peculiar plunk
into water, wonder of sliced apple
fed to me, dreamed storms, grass wet when I wake.

If even under the pine whose roots
choked out all other flowers,
the bleeding-heart came back, then

when light cuts across the composition
as at this season, hour, and latitude
it must, nothing is lost on it: linen
scarf framing a face tilted to one side,
candle-grayed plaster, gold brocade curtain,
shallow coin-sized bronze pans poised on a hand-
held balance, tabletop, pearls pouring down
the side of a box, half-sleeves, ermine-trimmed.
Which is to say there is nothing that light
does not love. Certainly nothing of her:
how her half-closed eyelids reiterate
her belly's crescent and her forehead's curve,
how her hand on the table seems to float.
That neck. That chin. Both forearms. Each finger.

**If a Babylonian astronomical diary
in cuneiform on a clay tablet
records the observation of Halley's Comet
in September of 164 BCE, then**

why not say *cluster of leaves still clinging*
to the tip of one branch (the others bare
that bloomed crimson last week) slowly turning
red to brown, rather than name the lover
who is not here? Why not *bored boy sitting*
on his front steps, sun going down over
the duplex across the street, white siding
letting direct sun send it shades whiter?
Why not savor this porch, call this warm day
girl measuring her front yard, heel to toe,
obsolete antenna on a chimney,
dry leaves in drifts beneath a parked Volvo,
trees trimmed at the top. Why not love the way
even her absence shines, and rustles so?

If the maple in the neighbor's yard
needs trimming, its branches having grown
against the slant of his roof, then

birds first of all: copper-feathered pheasant
collared white, with one curled plume for a crest;
a black-trimmed stork's arced wings and awkward flight;
one sparrow with gold cheeks and a striped breast.
My task today in place of purpose: list
what the world offers me when it withholds
you. Bushes bare of leaves but still aburst
with red berries. Green fields freckled by moles.
One woman standing on a stool, washing
windows; one with a poodle the exact
color of her own hair; two men watching
out a window; one woman shaking out
a rug; a small boy, crying, not waving
at the train so much as reaching for it.

If after her sixth pair of tusks
an elephant dies of starvation,
and if the ants that protect
the whistling acacia
also eat holes in its leaves, then

I will watch for you at the front window
whether or not you are due to arrive.
I once thought I could promise, even know.
I affirmed only what I could believe,
so I believed as much as I could. Now
I want what can't be true, what I must live
under, in a wide field the one shadow,
defying lightning, living a reprieve.
I name you *Ulmus suberosa*
for the improbability of your
standing there, for the fact that you will stay
if and as long as some will another
might call miracle or fate makes it so,
gives you to feed my guardian hunger.

If the tattooed woman ahead of me
in the checkout line, helping her husband
transfer groceries from the cart
to the conveyor, wore a long
red ribbon laced through a dozen gold rings
pierced in rows down her exposed back, then

I name you Playing Otter for the way
you walk through snow as if you had never,
as if — so it is — nothing lasts the day,
not least your sleek-skinned self, made for water,
made for swimming, sliding on your belly
down snow-slick embankments and out over
what was beaver pond but not ice yesterday
and may be back to scrub next winter.
We learn from snow ways to know exposed rock,
slanted strata shown by what brief white clings,
transient glazed texture wept from each crack,
crystalline score for what Aurora sings,
the glittering, against our normal lack,
of lovely, otherwise faraway things.

What is always possible is to go deeper into one's own sources, the body
and the ancient religious poetry.

According To H.

Many others having presumed
    to offer account
of how what had to happen did,
    taking care to keep
intact as much testimony
    as they can from those
who say they saw what we all wish
    we could say we'd seen,
I felt obliged, Theophilus,
    to pass along this
I love of what I can't believe.

The Mother of the Mother of God

Anna's sighs drew her eyes upward.
Spying in tangled laurel limbs between herself and heaven
a sparrow's nest, she sang to invoke the angel.

I was born to be hazed and cursed,
harried from the house of worship.
I am not like the birds of the air
that brood over hatchlings until they fly.
I am no doe, nose to the breezes,
ears raised, afraid for her fern-hidden fawn.
I am no sun-warmed tidal pool
teeming with algae, urchin, starfish, crab.
I am not a fire from which ash flies
to nourish next year's wheat in the neighbor's field.

What I bear, I bear not as a child but as a gift.

From Mary's Childhood

When the priest placed her on the third step of the altar
god graced her with grace and she danced her praise.
Doted on as doves are doted on, desert be damned,
she ate, when she ate, from the hand of an angel.

Lineage

He was neither young nor old
when he began to do what he did.

He was born, they say, to one
Joe (a pilgrim, an everyman),

himself the child of Will Likely
(born on a cold night in a tiny

house just off a gravel road,
silo-shadowed and barn-bruised),

child of Birdie Moulton,
child of Trusty McJunkin,

of what one would take back who can't,
whose fiancé seemed a saint

but whose husband proved otherwise,
child of fists clenched and voices raised,

child of that special place beside
a river in afternoon shade

now buried under brown water
a dam means to keep forever,

child of a boy named Beane and a girl
he didn't love but what the hell,

child of it was late and I was drunk
and he looked good, child of didn't think,

child of the ice storm, child of got
'tween asleep and wake, child of why not,

child of the flowering flowering plum,
child of David, child of Abraham.

One Approach

Setting out, they approached a place
where bandits often kidnapped victims
and stole their goods. The robbers heard
a motorcade, its sirens and motorcycles,
and they ran away. When the victims
saw only Joseph and Mary coming, they asked,
Where's the boss? Our attackers heard
his approach, and when they fled we escaped.
Mary answered them: *He will come after us.*

One Sparrow

Until he clapped his hands we could not fly,
but all we know now we already knew
from the moment his fingers touched the clay.

He talked to himself, narrated his play,
named all twelve of us. All we could do
was wait til his clapped hands taught us to fly.

We did wait, heard that old man scold the boy,
would have held our breaths had we the lungs to,
but til his fingers touched, we were still clay.

Making us had kept his sabbath holy:
birds out of clay supersedes any law,
and we knew when he clapped his hands we'd fly.

I was the third made, thrilled with my body,
thrilled soon to fly, but thrilled most that I *saw*
from the moment his fingers touched the clay.

The men were amazed and went away
to tell others, who would doubt it was true
that when the boy clapped his hands we could fly,
though *we* knew the moment he touched the clay.

Zacchaeus the Teacher, Shamed

This child speaks from some other world.
I beg you to take him away.

He knows letters as we cannot.
His gaze is too severe to bear.
Please, my brother, take him away.

He knows letters we do not know,
and how to spell out worlds with them.
I cannot understand his speech.

Who knows what belly bore this boy
who was born before earth was born,
whose words neither begin nor end.
I understood speech, until his.

I have been deceiving myself,
thinking I could be a teacher.
Take the boy away, my brother.
How could I even meet his eye?
Whatever he is — angel, god —
I do not know what I should say.

Before our earth was born, he was.
He knows how letters spell our world.
I beg you, take the boy away
before I burn in his strict gaze.

I know not what belly bore him.
It is not mine to say his name.
What should I call him? angel? god?
How should I look him in the face?

I have fooled myself until now.
The child speaks of another world
more our world than our world itself.
I dare not look him in the face.
What begins, begins in his words.

Which of us understands his speech?
Who has a gaze severe enough?
Who knows our world the way he knows?

My fear begs you take him away.
I understand this from his words:
I have fooled myself until now.

Beatitudes

Once the crowd grew, he withdrew to the rise.
To those students who followed him he said:
Replete are the breathless; theirs are the skies.
Replete, those who grieve, who must be consoled.
Replete, who stake no claim; all earth is theirs.
Replete, the fairness-famished; they'll be fed.
Replete, those who give mercy to others.
Replete, the transparent; seen, they see god.
Replete, those who make peace where there were wars.
Replete, all who suffer for doing good.
Replete you will be despite those jealous
of your repletion, themselves depleted.
Savor their slanders. Their forgotten fathers
slandered the prophets whose truths we remember.

Light

All our eyes saw, we saw as god sees it.
Not the glow that is god, but all it lit.

Miracles

When they saw a man blind from birth begging,
they asked, *Who failed, this man or his parents?*
He replied, *Seek not cause but occasion.*
He spat, made a paste of dust and spittle,
molded it over the blind man's eyelids,
and sent him to wash in Siloam's pool.

•

Even as waves broke over the boat,
lightning showed him still asleep in the stern,
and they marvelled at one not subject to storms.

•

When the crowd found him on the other shore,
he said to them, *You seek me not because
my words sustain you but because I gave
you back more bread than you had brought. Go,
find bread within yourselves, among yourselves.*

Parables

What he said, he said only as parables.
Why light a lamp, he asked, but then hide it?
Placed on a table, it lights the whole room,
and those with sight see all that can be seen.

> •

A man prepared a feast and invited friends,
but each met his invitation with some excuse:
Just bought some property, need to check it out.
New BMW, need to break it in.
My new lover's in town, just for the weekend.
So he had his help bring in from the streets
homeless persons, disfigured, disabled, blind,
who gladly filled his home and shared his food.

> •

A vintner with two children said to her son,
Put in some work today in the vineyard.
Sure, he said, but didn't leave the couch all day.
To her daughter she gave the same charge. *No way*,
the daughter said, but later went and worked.

> •

A wife was beaten often by her husband.
Every week or two, a few more bruises.
The other soccer moms tried not to notice.
Her pastor urged her to obedience.
The tattooed punk in the next cubicle
found out how to get her and her daughter
into a shelter, took time off from work

to drive them there in his old car, and gave
the shelter something from his check each month.

> •

One woman led her sunday school class in prayer:
Thank you, God, for giving us salvation
and for promising us eternal life.
Another, alone in her room, not knowing
who to call on, wept: *Help me, please, help me.*

> •

If only he had known in advance the thieves' plans,
his home would not have been broken into.

> •

A dying man willed his son the fallow field
his father had willed him. The son sold the land.
The buyer, plowing it in spring, unearthed a cache
long buried there, and now owns much more land.

> •

A moving company was short on help.
Going early to the unemployment line
the manager hired hands to help for the day.
He went again mid-morning, then again
at lunch, and one more time mid-afternoon.
At the end of the day, he had H.R.
pay each a hundred bucks. Those hired first complained.
Friend, he countered to their spokesperson, *what's wrong?*
I've been fair and honest with you, paying
the full amount we agreed to. Why begrudge
my being generous with someone else?

•

A real estate broker joined the Peace Corps
for a year. To each of his staff he gave charge
of a part of his assets, entrusting
to one a million dollars, to another
half a million, and to the last half that.
Upon return, he called each to account.
With your million, the first told him, *I bought
prime property that's worth two million now.*
The broker said, *Good work; you're promoted.*
The second said, *Your half million purchased
prime property that's worth a million now.*
The broker said, *Good work; you're promoted.*
The last employee said, *I know you're prudent.
The market looked like it was on a bubble.
I kept you in cash, you didn't lose a dime.*
The broker fired him and gave the money
to the first staff member to invest.

•

Though its seed be tiny, mustard, tended,
grows large enough for birds to nest in.

•

A sower scattered seed. What fell on the path
birds ate. What fell among rock grew quickly,
but in such shallow soil died the first dry spell.
What fell among weeds the weeds choked out.
What fell on good soil grew and brought forth grain,
enough for this year's bread plus next year's seed.

•

A widow whose husband had given her
over the years a dozen different rings
lost one of them. For a week she moved chairs,
emptied the vacuum cleaner bag, lost sleep,
cleaned cabinets, pulled clothes from dresser drawers.
When she found the ring, she had her best friends
in for dinner to help her celebrate.

75

•

A rancher had two sons. The younger asked
for his inheritance — he wanted out.
The father sold half his land and half his stock.
The son moved to the city, tried college,
drank a lot, played pool and poker, slept late,
went to parties, met women, bought them nice clothes,
drove a Viper for a while, then a 'Vette.
When the money ran out, he washed dishes,
did go-fer work at a construction site,
sold his car to pay off credit card debt,
and figured out he'd be better back at home:
at least the ranch hands have a roof and get fed.
He hitchhiked home, and hadn't hit the door
before his father tearfully embraced him.
The son had prepared his speech: *I screwed up.*
I'm not your son. Hire me back as a hand.
The father got him decent jeans and boots,
had half the county in to share a steer.
The older son was angry: *I helped here*
the whole time he was throwing money at cars
and whiskey and whores, and you never gave
a party for me. The father replied,
Son, we've shared work and weather. All I have
is yours. But it's right to celebrate now:
your brother who was lost to us has been found;
my son who was dead lives with us again.

•

All he told them, he told as parables.
A woman, he said, mixed just a little yeast
in with the flour, and the whole loaf rose.

76

Agrapha

Near me, near fire. Far from me, orphaned in darkness and cold.

It is a small thing, an easy thing, to forfeit one's soul.

One proud man can clutter continents.

Trouble itself is far from god; a soul in trouble is near god.

Nothing matters less than what you call god, or matters more.

A man missed the call, listening for his name.

It doesn't matter whether you *believe* I speak from another world.

Kerygma

Even during the watch of Elijah
there walked widows enough across a land
starved by stingy skies, crusted in parched soil,
but he was sent to only one of them,
a widow in Sidon named Sarepta.
Of all the lepers in Elisha's time
only Naaman the Syrian was healed.

·

Is it so hard to understand
that corruption does not enter
from outside but arises from within?

·

How can you fail to grasp
that when I speak of bread
I do not mean bread?

·

I tell you, Elijah *has* come.

Mercies

They said to him, *The law insists on stones.*
Ignoring them, he knelt, scribbling in dust.
They said again, *The law insists on stones.*
His finger kept moving across the dust.

      •

Simon, you see this woman.
You gave me no water for my feet,
but she washed them with her tears
and wiped them with her own hair.
You gave me no kiss to welcome me,
but she has not stopped kissing my feet.
You did not anoint my head
but she has anointed my feet.
To *her* I say, *Take respite. Be whole.*
You are reunited with yourself.

Hymn

Before his arrest by those who follow the lawless law of the snake,
having gathered us together he said, *Before I am handed over,*
join me in a hymn to the law that is law. Prepare to embrace
what awaits us. So we circled him and he said, *Respond amen to me.*

I will grow, and I will feed what grows. Amen.
I will imprison, and be imprisoned. Amen.
I will free, and be freed. Amen.
I will burn and burn, and I will be burned. Amen.
I will bear the burden borne by what bears me. Amen.
I will pierce, and be pierced. Amen.

  Grace that gives grace does so by dancing.

I would drown, had I not drowned already. Amen.
I would let go the hand that holds me, had I not fallen already. Amen.
I would forfeit my food to the hungry, had I not already starved. Amen.
I would carry earth's curvature, were not my own horizon so near. Amen.
I would singe treetops, blown branch to branch, were I not already ash. Amen.
I would stare down the sun, were I not already blind. Amen.
I would die for you, were I not already dead. Amen.

  What grace cannot give cannot be given.
  Dancing gives what even grace withholds.

When I listen, what I hear replaces love. Amen.
When I sing, my voice replaces faith. Amen.
When I dance, my body replaces grief. Amen.
I will listen if you will sing. Amen.
I will sing if you will dance. Amen.
I tell you the earth's movement is a dance. Amen.
I tell you knowledge is not knowledge, but dancing is. Amen.
Hope is not hope, but dancing is. Amen.
Time is not fire, but dancing is the stars. Amen.
God scorns sacrifices of barley and goats
but offer your hand and god may dance with you. Amen. And amen.

Spoken to Judas Thomas, Jesus' Twin

I am a serpent, son of a serpent,
corrupted son of a corrupted father,
son of one proud of his lies, proud of murders,
who killed the fourth brother by killing the third,
son of one who steals from those who only borrow,
who encircles the globe, takes his tail in his mouth.
I am the serpent who slithered into Eden,
and said to Eve exactly what god said to say,
the serpent at whose call Cain killed his closest kin.
Through me are sown thorns and thistles to choke out corn.
I cast down angels, bound them to earth by desire,
I fed Pharaoh such willfulness that harm
to his enemies also brought harm to his own,
I whispered to Caiaphas his lie to Pilate,
I prompted Judas. I hold your place in the abyss.

Passions

Peter, James, and John, Sleeping:
You watch for betrayal, we betray it.

Sarra:
You must kill the lawless to reveal the law.

Judas:
Lead him away, for his own safety.

Malchos:
The literal is the lesser loss.

Peter:
Now neither of us knows him, you nor I.

Pilate:
Every crowd wishes to harm itself.

Barabbas:
I acted; he spoke, a more heinous crime.

Gestas:
My petty claims still curse your pompous ones.

The Centurion:

Where should we see god if not in a death?

Joseph of Arimathea:

Light cannot be buried in a cave.

Veronica:

On this thin fabric, my blood, his image.

Mary Magdalene, Mary the Mother of James, and Salome:

Words sound different, coming from an angel.

Cleopas:

Did not our very viscera burn?

Letter

I write you in grief.
My Herodias,
my loving daughter,
skating on the ice,
fell through to her neck,
and when her mother
trying to save her
grasped her head, she was
decapitated,
and the water swept
her body away.
Now my cold wife holds
the head on her knees
and fills this whole house
with fevered keening.

I worry over
the death of Jesus,
the scale of my sins:
killing the Baptist,
slaughtering children.
When you see Jesus,
intercede for me
as the prophets say
you will, and must.

Lesbonax my son
wastes away, and I
suffer from dropsy;
worms come from my mouth.
My wife has blinded
her own left eye by
constant sobbing.
God makes no errors.
We do nothing right.
Sorrow has come to
the Jews and the priests,
the children of light
fallen to darkness.

Since we are one age,
Pilate, I beg you
bury my children,
bury me, my wife
with what honor god
and justice allow.
Better your hand than
a priest's, to crumble
the first clod onto
my coffin. Farewell.
I enclose my wife's
earrings and my own
signet ring. I'll need
neither in the grave.

Even in this world
judgment has begun,
but I fear the judgment
of the next world more.
This, temporary;
that, everlasting.

Conclusion

Beyond what's written here, much else might be.
Of the word that is its own beginning
the world could not contain books enough.

Protevangelium

I, Harvey, wrote this history
    here in the mountains
while tumult raged in the desert.
    I had to see snow,
though which evoked this history —
    the desert, the snow —
I don't know. I praise what I can,
    as I am able,
and solicit a miracle
    I must not expect:
from my emptiness, history,
    from history, grace.

Books from Etruscan Press

A Poetics of Hiroshima | William Heyen

Saint Joe's Passion | J. D. Schraffenberger

American Fugue | Alexis Stamatis

Drift Ice | Jennifer Atkinson

The Widening | Carol Moldaw

Parallel Lives | Michael Lind

God Bless: A Political/Poetic Discourse | H. L. Hix

Chromatic | H. L. Hix (National Book Award finalist)

The Confessions of Doc Williams & Other Poems | William Heyen

Art into Life | Frederick R. Karl

Shadows of Houses | H. L. Hix

The White Horse: A Colombian Journey | Diane Thiel

Wild and Whirling Words: A Poetic Conversation | H. L. Hix

Shoah Train | William Heyen (National Book Award finalist)

Crow Man | Tom Bailey

As Easy As Lying: Essays on Poetry | H. L. Hix

Cinder | Bruce Bond

Free Concert: New and Selected Poems | Milton Kessler

September 11, 2001: American Writers Respond | William Heyen

etruscan press
www.etruscanpress.org

Etruscan Press books may be ordered from:

Consortium Book Sales and Distribution
800-283-3572
www.cbsd.com

Small Press Distribution
800-869-7553
www.spdbooks.com